THE HASIDIM

Other books by Ira Moskowitz

American Indian Ceremonial Dances

Great Paintings of All Time

Isaac Bashevis Singer's latest novel

Enemies, a Love Story

THE HASIDIM

Paintings, Drawings, and Etchings by
IRA MOSKOWITZ

Text by
ISAAC BASHEVIS SINGER
and the Artist

CROWN PUBLISHERS, INC., NEW YORK

Acknowledgments

Thanks are gratefully given to Moses Moskowitz, the artist's brother, for his assistance in the translation of *Hasidism and the Artist*; to Anna Barry Moskowitz, the artist's wife, and to Joseph Winston whose advice and support helped make this book possible.

Library of Congress Catalog Card Number: 72–84288
ISBN: 0-517-500477
Printed in the United States of America

Published simultaneously in Canada by General Publishing Company Limited

To the artist's grandfather,
Grand Rabbi Shalom Hakohen Jolles of Stryj,
of blessed memory

Contents

THE SPIRIT
OF JEWISHNESS

BY ISAAC BASHEVIS SINGER

As I'm writing this I see before me pictures of religious Jews in the Williamsburg section of Brooklyn, as well as a number of sketches and lithographs of Hasidic Jews in Israel prepared by my friend Ira Moskowitz. I see fur-edged rabbinical hats, long gaberdines, big beards, sidelocks, women in wigs and in bonnets that were already obsolete even in my youth in Warsaw. I know that thousands of Jews and non-Jews who see these people want to know: What does this signify? Are they all rabbis? Does it say anywhere in the Torah or Talmud that Jews must dress this way? Do they belong to some special Jewish sect? Neither the Reform, the Conservative, nor even those Jews who attend Orthodox services dress this way—therefore, to what group do these people belong? And what is their reason for wearing clothes that make them so conspicuous?

It is even more astonishing to see Jews dressed this way driving trucks,

6

carrying bundles, or delivering goods. Among them are businessmen and workers. Since that is so, what reason is there for their rabbinical garb?

I must admit that I once shared similar feelings when I looked at nuns. Why the black and white habits, the shaven heads, the ankle-length garments? Did Jesus demand that his brides wear such uniforms? Was not religion a matter of the heart only? Would a long habit or a gaberdine serve as a guarantee against hate, envy, lust, glory-seeking, slander, and vengefulness?

I was often puzzled too when I saw pictures of Gandhi wrapped in a sheet. Similarly, the world was amazed nearly a century ago when Tolstoy suddenly donned a Russian peasant's smock. Why did he do this? Many people in and out of Russia accused him of exhibitionism or simply of publicizing himself, although they should have known better. No matter what he did he could not have made himself more famous than he already was.

Well then, what about the hippies in New York and in all the European cities who seem to have responded simultaneously to some silent command to grow long hair and beards, to neglect their clothes, and to associate with others as sloppy as themselves? Is this nothing more than a fad or does such attire disguise some idea?

People seldom realize that a style of dress, of hair, and of every kind of external nonconformity represents a sort of language, albeit frequently vague and unintelligible. So far, no one has compiled a dictionary of these "languages" nor researched their grammar and syntax. Nevertheless, they are forms of expression. Long hair, beards, and moustaches express meanings that short hair and clean-shaven upper lips and chins simply do not. A long garment "speaks" differently to us than does a short one. Languages themselves would have no significance if objects did not possess a speech of their own. World literature would be meaningless if the human spirit did not try to express itself in the most divergent possible ways. We are curious to see a celebrity because his face, his manners, his gestures, and his garments say things we cannot glean from his words and deeds only. Gandhi becomes much more understandable to us when we see his face and mode of dress. Tolstoy somehow would not seem the same without his patriarchal beard. We cannot imagine him looking like Lord Byron, nor Dostoevsky resembling Kaiser Wilhelm. It would somehow seem inappropriate. Bare souls undoubtedly exist somewhere, but the souls with which we are familiar have wrapped themselves in bodies, in clothes, and in manners.

Women are more sensitive to these "languages" and therefore place more emphasis on such externals as clothes, hairdos, and jewelry. A man will seldom criticize another man's choice of suit or tie but a woman will accurately analyze another's outfit and gather meaning from the way she dresses and fixes her hair. Homosexuals often dress exotically not only to facilitate recognition among themselves but out of a strong compulsion to express their personalities. Even people for whom it would be prudent to be inconspicuous, such as criminals, often dress in identifiable fashion. The Russian revolutionists of the nineteenth century all had good reason to remain anonymous; yet many of them let their hair grow long and wore wide-brimmed hats and red or black blouses with sashes and tassels. Today, the American radical frequently dresses somewhat differently than the conservative.

Besides expressing the human spirit, clothes and hair styles also hold a key to self-discipline. A priest may occasionally be tempted to ride a carousel and eat an ice-cream cone but he is not likely to do this while wearing his priestly garb. His very costume dictates that he conduct himself with dignity. A rabbi in a long cloak, a beard, and sidelocks is not likely to dally with a girl on a street corner. Tolstoy—by donning the peasant smock—forever precluded his attendance at the elaborate balls of the aristocracy that he described so well in his novels. Gandhi's attire kept him from becoming a man of the world. Clothes guard a person just as words do. Even if a nun got the urge to attend a nightclub her habit would keep her from fulfilling this whim. Religious people in all times were aware of the weaknesses inherent in man's nature. They knew that he is often more ashamed before his fellow human beings than before God. A person ready to betray the loftiest principle will still take pains not to appear laughable nor to make himself an object of other men's anger and scorn.

When the Jew was driven from his land he knew the peril that threatened his future existence—the necessity of mixing with strangers.

No exiled people has lasted as a group for more than a generation or two. But the Jew was determined to endure many generations of exile if necessary, to remain true to his God, to the Torah, and to his native land even though it lay in ruins and was occupied by strangers. It was an undertaking without counterpart in the history of mankind. It could only be effected thanks to a mighty discipline and a colossal mysticism of upbringing and education. The basis of this discipline was the total estrangement from the peoples among whom the Jew would dwell; not a physical estrangement but a spiritual one. True, the Jew was forced to do business with the gentile and often to work for him. But that was the extent of their association. The Jew had to erect a spiritual ghetto around himself that was immeasurably more isolated and impregnable than the physical ghetto to which he was later confined. To the Jew, the A to Z of his religion was the law of the Torah, as written in Leviticus 18:3: "After the doings of the land of Egypt, wherein ye dwelt, shall ye not do: and after the doings of the land of Canaan, whither I bring you, shall ye not do: neither shall ye walk in their ordinances."

If the gentile wore a short coat, he, the Jew, would wear a long one. If the gentile's hat was round, his would be pointed. According to the Talmud, the book of Jewish religious law, the Jew dared not even tie his shoelaces in the same way as his gentile neighbor. These laws were established not out of enmity toward the gentile but rather as a reminder for the Jew to adhere to certain conditions if he wanted to retain his identity for hundreds if not thousands of years. True they sometimes copied the fashions of their gentile neighbors but in all instances they lent their own touches to them.

The men of the Jewish version of the Enlightenment who wanted the Jews to take off their gaberdines and become Europeans often mocked the rigors that the rabbis had imposed upon the Jew through the generations. But all these laws and rigors were intended as shackles to curb the Jew from mixing with others. Assimilation is a natural process. A minority always seeks to fit itself into the majority. The weak will inevitably fashion themselves after the strong. The temptations were tremendous. Often the people among whom the Jews lived forced them to integrate. Romantic unions between Jews and gentiles were unavoidable. For hundreds and thousands of years the Jew forced himself to go against human nature.

The form of dress he adopted made this integration more difficult. He instinctively altered the language of his host nation so that it became his own dialect and seemed alien and comical to his neighbors. He shaved his daughter's hair and himself grew a beard and sidelocks that labeled him a Jew even from a distance.

History shows that the segregation between gentile and Jew was not uniform through the ages. It was less pronounced in the Arab lands than in the Christian, and even there variations existed in different times and in different places. The Italian and Spanish Jews spoke the native languages among themselves and had close relations with the inhabitants. The Jews in France, Germany, and eastern Europe were the most isolated from the native populations. It is almost a truism that wherever segregation was least severe assimilation was the strongest. It was axiomatic among Jews that once one of them made the slightest move to adjust his ways to those of the gentiles, that individual stood poised on the threshold of conversion. And Jews preferred to lose such a person completely than to retain him in their camp and chance his infecting other Jews with his ideas. The community boasted but one weapon: excommunication.

By cutting away from the community all those who broke the rules of spiritual segregation the Jew practiced a kind of selection which retained in the community only its most devout members. For centuries a Jew had but one choice—either to bear all the burdens of his faith or to go over completely to the religion of the majority. Assimilation in today's sense of the word was nonexistent. It only came about through Emancipation after the Napoleonic wars.

The Emancipation created a new type of Jew, one who could renounce the laws of his religion yet remain a Jew; or at least not go all the way toward conversion. This so-called worldly Jew was a riddle both to himself and to the Christian world. Since he disobeyed the laws of his religion, what constituted his allegiance to his faith? Some people of this kind called themselves national Jews. Their Jewishness consisted of belonging to a group or of speaking Yiddish or Hebrew. This modern Jew created Zionism and waged a struggle against anti-Semitism. His kind includes many who claim that even if they wanted to assimilate they would not be allowed to do so. Thus the worldly Jew who lives outside of Israel belongs to a group that has no land and often no language of its own, but shares common interests, character, and personality. The modern Jew's identity may not be defined in any dictionary, but it exists nevertheless.

The religious Jew, the pious one, does not believe in the national Jew or in his future. To him, a Jew without a religion is what he is to many non-Jews—an enigma, a mass of contradictions, a paradox. If the pious Jew of former times had to exert every effort to segregate himself from the gentile, today's pious Jews must redouble these efforts to remain apart not so much from gentiles as from the great number of nonreligious Jews or those who have tried to reform Jewishness. To the very pious Jews of Williamsburg those Jews who are Communists, freethinking Zionists, or members of Reform or Conservative congregations are all heretics and candidates for assimilation and mixed marriage. And they place in this same category those Jews in Israel who either don't practice Jewishness or try to reform it there. Since danger lurks for him both in and outside of his group, today's pious Jew must exercise a twofold vigilance. He is like a soldier caught up in a civil war—surrounded by enemies on all sides. Any effort to mitigate this or that rigor leads promptly to licentiousness and assimilation. Today's pious Jew must enforce ever-stricter and more rigorous measures in order to retain his historical role and to raise a generation that will follow in his ways.

Thus, if the worldly Jew dresses in short garments, the pious Jew must stick to his long gaberdine. Since the former shaves his beard and sidelocks, the latter must let them grow as long as possible. The worldly Jew has founded a number of organizations to protect Jewish interests but the pious Jew must keep far away from their activities. If a pious Jew must choose between entering a church or a Reform temple, Rabbi Moshe Sofer judged that he should rather enter the church—it represents less danger to him than does the temple where scrolls of the Torah are kept and where people allegedly pray to the Jewish God. A new kind of segregation has been established among the most pious Jews—a segregation from the modern Jew and his institutions. All the efforts of these Jews are now bent to this end.

Nor is there unity among the pious themselves. They too are divided into factions both in Israel and in the lands of the Diaspora. Those belonging to the Mizrachi are willing to work with the modern Jews and their organizations. Those of the Agudas Israel, on the other hand, stay at a greater distance from the nonbelieving Jews, but they recognize the state of Israel and have representatives in the Knesset and often in the ruling government. Those Jews stand ready to work alongside heretic Jews just as pious Jews have had to consort with gentiles throughout history. The fact is that heretic Jews are very able and have set up the various funds which have made the Jewish state possible. To ignore them entirely would often be impracticable. So even the members of Agudas Israel have made numerous compromises. Many have donned short garments; others have trimmed beards and sidelocks. When the Germans began to make reparation payments to victims of Nazi persecution, the members of the Agudas Israel at first grimaced and called it blood money as despicable as idolatry. Later they relented. The gentile may be *tref* but his money is kosher. They applied this same principle to the "Jewish goy."

But the extremists of Orthodoxy—the Szatmar Hasidim (who came from Hungary to the United States) and the Naturei Karta (watcher of the city of Jerusalem) in Israel—those Jews in the fur-edged hats and high stockings—still contend that every step nearer to the modern Jew, no matter how small, is the path to corruption. It is not out of malice that the Szatmar rabbi calls the members of the Agudas Israel heretics and men of evil. The ultraorthodox Jew adheres to the principle that once the movement toward the other side is launched, total homogeneity can only be a matter of time.

What is the number of these extremists? Not large. Throughout the whole world it comes to perhaps 100,000. These Jews have never recognized the Jewish state. In Israel, they do not cast votes nor have representatives in the Knesset. They do not speak the modern Hebrew but stick to the Yiddish of their grandfathers and great-grandfathers. They have rejected modern Jewishness and isolated themselves just as their ancestors isolated themselves from Spinoza and Uriel Acosta. The ultraorthodox Jews have unofficially excommunicated the modern Jew, although they themselves constitute a small minority among the world Jewry. To them, we all are branches broken off from the Jewish trunk. They are convinced that our future is the obliteration of our Jewishness. They, few as they are, will maintain the yoke of our religion. They, the extremists, will be there to receive the Messiah.

Are they right or do they represent an ossified sector of the Jewish community, an anachronism that time will disperse? Only history will tell. One thing is clear—their way of life is based on a profound religious logic and a historic reason. The long beards and sidelocks, the old-fashioned garments, and the clinging to all the rigors and customs are directed toward one purpose only—complete segregation from the gentile, and even more from the Jew who is heading toward ultimate disappearance. This segregation is as old as Jewish exile itself and has maintained the Jew through the two thousand years of his existence in the Diaspora.

THE SPIRIT OF HASIDISM

BY ISAAC BASHEVIS SINGER

Like all so-called new movements, Hasidism was, in fact, based on ancient tradition. Deeply rooted in Jewish religious life, it reached its zenith at a time when the Jewish Enlightenment, the current of assimilation and secularization, first began to make its way from Germany and western Europe into the countries of eastern Europe.

Hasidism was a reaction to a series of upheavals that struck the Jews in Poland, where they had been living even before the days of King Casimir the Great, who reigned from 1333 to 1370. In the mid-seventeenth century, the Cossack revolts under Bogdan Chmielnicki brought bloody persecutions to the Polish and Ukrainian Jews that could compare in brutality to the massacres perpetrated by Hitler three centuries later. The Cossack outrages and their repercussions set the stage for the advent of the false messiahs—Sabbatai Zvi (1626–1676) and Jacob Frank (1726?–

1791)—who attracted thousands of followers. When Sabbatai Zvi embraced Islam in order to escape death at the hands of the Turks, some of his adherents followed him into the mosques. Even larger numbers of his disciples, such as the Donmehs of Izmir, went through the formalities of conversion to the Islamic faith but secretly remained loyal to Sabbatai Zvi's version of Judaism. A century later Jacob Frank led many of his followers to the baptismal font; he believed that Jews could gain salvation by apostasy.

Judaism managed to survive that era of disruption from within and persecution from without, primarily because of the ghetto, which insulated Jews against alien influences, and because of the institution of the *herem* (ecclesiastical excommunication), which enabled the Jewish communities to deal effectively with the dissidents in their midst. The Jews of the Diaspora refused to make allowances for those who had turned aside even one step from the path of tradition. In Judaism quality took precedence over quantity; depth of religious commitment was considered more important than sheer numbers. Anyone who rejected so much as one precept of the Shulhan Arukh, the basic code of Jewish law, automatically placed himself outside the Jewish camp.

The rise of the Haskalah, the Jewish Enlightenment, in the latter part of the eighteenth century, however, created a new situation. It was impossible simply to exclude the Maskilim, the enlightened ones, as the followers of Haskalah were known, from the Jewish fold, first because they were so numerous, and second, because most of them refused to abandon Judaism. Their aim was not to leave Judaism but to reform it. They created Jewish communities of their own and in many instances gave badly needed economic help to their Orthodox brethren.

It appeared that the Enlightenment was the trend of the future. Religion was losing its firm grip not only upon the peoples among whom the Jews were living, but also upon the Jews themselves. The French Revolution, the Emancipation, the advances of industry and science, and the social and educational reforms presented challenges to the Jews for which nothing in all their previous history had prepared them. It was one thing to fight against religious dissidents, but it was quite another to answer those who urged the Jews to learn the language of the countries in which they lived, to adopt modern dress, and to put an end to the existence of the *luftmensch* (literally, one who lives on air; one without a trade or gainful employment), the filth, the isolation, and such old-fashioned practices as marrying off their young children.

Given the times and circumstances, it was not surprising that the Haskalah soon attracted a wide following, particularly among the younger generation. After the excitement and the atmosphere of adventure created by Sabbatai Zvi and Jacob Frank, life in the little Jewish villages had become even more bleak and dull than before. The would-be Messiahs had proven false, and there was no reason to believe that the true Messiah, whom the Jews had been awaiting for close to eighteen centuries, might not tarry for yet another eighteen hundred years. The rabbis and the scholars, who had never been more than a minority in Jewry, no longer had the same power over their people as before. All they could do was threaten their congregations with the fires of Gehenna.

It was in this setting that Hasidism emerged. Hasidism did not seek to change the Jewish faith; it merely sought to effect a change in the attitude of the Jew toward his religion. It remained true to Jewish tradition and to the Shulhan Arukh, but it introduced some new and refreshing elements into Jewish living. Hasidism was a movement of the masses. It accepted anyone who sought it out and rejected no one; it welcomed the unlearned and even the females, who previously could expect little more than to serve as footstools to their husbands in Paradise. Many Hasidic rebbes received women in audience and listened to their troubles—no small achievement. Legend has it that when Israel Baal Shem (1700–c.1760), the founder of Hasidism, danced with his followers, he permitted his daughter Hodel to dance together with the men.

Hasidism essentially sprang from the same soil that brought forth the false Messiahs. It was rooted in the Kabbalah, particularly the Kabbalah of Rabbi Isaac Luria (1534–1572), or Ari, the lion, as he is called.

Some of the teachings of the Kabbalah may well be as old as Judaism itself. Biblical literature makes reference to angels, seraphs, cherubim, sacred animals in heaven, and even to conjuring up the souls of the dead. The Talmud is replete with accounts of heavenly mansions and the sort of magic that is found in the Kabbalah. However, the mystical teachings of the Kabbalah first spread to wider circles through the *Zohar,* the authorship of which tradition ascribes to Rabbi Simeon ben Yohai, who taught in Palestine during the second century, but modern scholarship holds that it is the work of Rabbi Moses de Leon, a mystic who lived in Spain in the thirteenth century.

The Kabbalah never gained unanimous acceptance among the Jews. Indeed, it has encountered vehement opposition in many Jewish circles. According to the Kabbalah, all the worlds in the universe are emanations of the godhead. Not only living creatures, but also inanimate objects developed from the Divine substance. In effect, God created the world from His own essence. It was not easy to reconcile this pantheistic doctrine with the fundamentals of Judaism. The Kabbalists had to reinterpret many religious principles to accommodate them to the ideas contained in their mystic lore.

The last and the greatest of the early Kabbalists was Rabbi Isaac Luria. He emphasized the doctrine of *tzimtzum,* in which God had to subdue His power and to dim His infinite light before He could create the universe. Without this act creation would have been impossible because the light that emanates from God would have engulfed the universe and caused it to disintegrate. Creation, like a painting by an artist, must have both lights and shadows. These shadows are the source of all evil and the powers that hold creation together. When God created the world he had to create evil. Without evil there would be no virtue and sin, free choice and reward.

The Ari—or, more accurately, his disciple, Rabbi Haim Vital (1543–1620), who noted down the teachings of his master—was the author of *Etz Hachayim* ("The Tree of Life"), which explains Luria's Kabbalah. The Kabbalah is, and has always been, esoteric in nature. The truths contained in it were intended only for the few.

The adherents of the two false Messiahs and the early Hasidim were all believers in the Kabbalah, but with one fundamental difference. The followers of Sabbatai Zvi and the Frankists were so enamored of the Kabbalah that they rejected many laws and precepts of the Bible and the Talmud. They believed that the Kabbalah had superseded the law of Moses. The Baal Shem and his pupils, on the other hand, considered the Kabbalah as an addition to, but not as a replacement for, the Torah. Also, the Hasidim felt that the Kabbalah should not remain the property of a small group of initiates, but should be made known to all Jews.

To the Hasidim, the strict observance of Jewish law in itself was not enough. The important thing was the *kavanah,* the intense concentration that can make a man oblivious to his physical surroundings while praying or performing a religious act. Furthermore, the test of true service to God was whether it was carried out in a spirit of joy. He who was sad proved by his very sadness that he lacked genuine faith in the Creator. *Simcha shel Mitzvah,* the joy inherent in religious observance, is the very core of Hasidism. Baruch Spinoza, the seventeenth-century pantheist, had preached a love of God founded on reason, *Amor dei Intellectualis.* The Hasidim, by contrast, taught that God must be loved, above all, with the heart. He who truly loved God, they asserted, could not be anything else but happy and full of hope.

The Orthodox opponents of Hasidism warned that Hasidism was not based on true Judaism but was a form of Sabbatai Zvi worship or perhaps even Frankism in disguise. The leader of the Mitnagdim (Opponents), Rabbi Elijah ben Shlomo, the saintly Gaon of Vilna (1720–1797), went so far as to pronounce a ban on Hasidism and to excommunicate its followers.

Nevertheless, the Hasidic movement spread rapidly, and when the Haskalah came to eastern Europe, the fervor of Hasidism proved a potent antidote against its cold rationalism. The Enlightenment stressed the importance of being practical, of obtaining a secular education, and of adopting the ways of the modern world. The Hasidim, on the other hand, maintained that one touch of joy in the service of God was worth more than all secular accomplishments or even than the diligent study of Jewish law carried out without fervor.

In order to sustain the spirit of gladness, the Hasidim declared that Jews had to live, or at least to meet as often as possible, with a *tzaddik,* a "righteous man," whom they could accept as their spiritual leader. A spiritual leader could only be one who was able to establish a soul-to-soul rapport with his followers. And since the needs of soul differed from individual to individual, each Hasid had to find a *tzaddik,* or rebbe, whose guidance he would feel able to follow because he would sense that this man's soul responded to the most profound yearnings of his own.

A glance at the leaders who became known as *tzaddikim,* or rebbes, in the early Hasidic movement shows a varied group of personalities. Israel Baal Shem, who was in fact the original rebbe of Hasidism, was a humble man who appealed to the simple folk because he was one of their own. His favorite disciple and spiritual heir, Reb Dov Baer of Meseritz (1710–1772), was a little more sophisticated and was widely respected for his knowledge of the Torah. Another disciple of Baal Shem, Rabbi Jacob Joseph of Polonnoye, represented a synthesis of Talmudic erudition and Hasidic passion. Each rebbe drew to his "court" Hasidim of his own type and inclination. Thus, there developed around the rebbes—and the "dynasties" that they begot—various distinct schools of Hasidism. The Hasidim of Kozienice and Lizhensk (Lezajsk) were renowned for their piety; the rabbi of Lublin, Reb Bunim of Przysucha, and the rebbe of Kotzk attracted men of wit and wisdom; the followers of Reb Menahem Mendel of Vitebsk and Reb Israel of Ruzhin often combined piety with worldly affluence.

The great luminary of the Hasidic world during the late eighteenth and early nineteenth centuries was Rabbi Nachman of Bratzlav, a great-grandson of the Baal Shem. Reb Nachman, who was less than forty years old when he died in 1811, united in his personality extraordinary erudition, impassioned love of God, and a quality that might be characterized as holy hysteria. His grave in the Russian city of Uman and the small chapel built over the site became a place of pilgrimage for thousands of fervent Hasidim until it was razed by the Communists. Rabbi Nachman's teachings contained profound religious and psychological insights. The prayers he composed express all the yearnings of the religious spirit. His famous tales are among the world's great folkloric masterpieces.

Reb Nachman had not only ardent friends and disciples but also some bitter enemies, even in the Hasidic world. A number of rebbes attacked him to the point where he was nearly excommunicated. Reb Nachman complained that his enemies had "invented a man and then proceeded to hate him," but the blame may not have been entirely on his adversaries. Reb Nachman himself frequently expressed ridicule and contempt for the mediocrities who were beginning to claim the title of rebbe in his day. He was too brilliant and too sensitive to be tolerant of pettiness.

Just as Rabbi Haim Vital acted as scribe and interpreter to his master, Rabbi Isaac Luria, so Reb Nachman left to his disciple, Rabbi Nathan of Nemirov, the task of writing down his teachings for posterity. While, in the case of Rabbi Vital, it was often difficult to say which of the thoughts set down in *Etz Hachayim* were his master's and which his own, Rabbi Nathan had no other ambition but to serve his great mentor and to note down exactly his words of Divine wisdom.

In 1798 Reb Nachman visited the Holy Land. It was the fulfillment of his lifelong dream. Such a journey entailed hardships and perils. There is reason to believe that Reb Nachman was then already suffering from tuberculosis, the disease that would kill him thirteen years later. The brief account of his pilgrimage is of enormous psychological interest. Reb Nachman seems to have had a feeling that all the forces of evil had banded together to prevent him from making this voyage, which he believed might end the Exile and bring the Messiah. Perhaps he believed that he himself was destined to become the redeemer.

During its early days, the most bitter opponents of the movement were the rabbis who feared that Hasidism might give rise to a new sect of dissidents. In time, however, the rabbinic world realized that traditional Judaism had nothing to fear from the Hasidim. Many even came to welcome the warmth that Hasidism had brought into Jewish tradition.

But Hasidism was confronted by a new and highly articulate foe, the Haskalah—the Enlightenment. As the Maskilim saw it, Hasidism was a pernicious influence because it kept hundreds of thousands of Jews in Poland and Russia from progress. The Haskalah literature of the early nineteenth century is full of mockery for the Hasidim and their rebbes. Israel Axenfeld (1787–1866), a mediocre writer of plays and novels in Russia, ridiculed the teachings of Reb Nachman of Bratzlav and satirized him cruelly. Axenfeld preached logic, good grammar, modern hygiene and, above all, the importance of being practical and worldly.

The disciples of Haskalah especially attacked the folk beliefs of the east European Jews and their tales of demons, evil spirits, dybbuks, transmigrations of the soul, and miracle-working saints. Like their counterparts in Germany and Austria, the early Maskilim of eastern Europe disdained the Yiddish language, which they called "jargon" or "the maidservant."

Before long, however, many of the Maskilim realized that even if the Jews were to adopt modern clothing, secular education, and the Russian or Polish language, they would never gain the acceptance of the Russian or Polish people. As a matter of fact, nineteenth-century anti-Semitism throughout Europe aimed its attacks more at "modern" Jews than at those who remained loyal to their religion. The Jew was no longer hated as an infidel, an enemy of the Church, but as a rival who was threatening to take over the trades and professions of his Christian neighbors. He was also feared as an instigator of world revolution. Poverty-stricken Jews in Czarist Russia were easy prey for the revolutionary movement. Many young Jews honestly believed that the revolution would sweep away every barrier of class, nationality, and religion, so that all men everywhere would truly become brothers. To them revolution itself became a religion.

A number of the Maskilim who were less imbued with revolutionary zeal and were becoming increasingly disenchanted with life in Russia urged their fellow Jews to emigrate, particularly to the United States. Other Maskilim, of more romantic bent, began to talk of a return to Palestine where the Jews would become a nation like all other nations. These disciples of "enlightenment" became ardent lovers of biblical literature and developed an admiration for the Hebrews of the Bible. They pointed out that the Jews of biblical times had not been pious paupers and timid creatures with bent backs, but were tillers of the soil and warriors. They were in many ways like the gentiles whom the Maskilim sought to emulate. Back in Palestine, the Jews would straighten their backs, cast off the yoke of Talmudic and Hasidic "superstition," and return to nature and to the soil. Writers of this brand of Haskalah, such as Abraham Mapu (1808–1867), produced romantic novels of life in ancient Palestine, where young men and maidens danced together and made love.

The Haskalah was winning new and significant victories all the time. By the middle of the nineteenth century Hasidism was experiencing the same fate that sooner or later comes to all movements: it had begun to stagnate. The descendants of the earlier rebbes lacked the vitality and the charisma of their ancestors. The Haskalah was vigorously promoting its political Zionism and the modernization of the Hebrew language. Jews in western Europe and in the United States had attained important positions in the arts, the sciences, the professions, and even government service. Enlightened young Jews were pioneers in agricultural settlements in Palestine. Secular Jews did not consider themselves bound together by a common religion, but by an ethnic and cultural heritage.

The attitude of the "modernists" toward Hasidism began to soften only after it had become clear that Haskalah had taken firm roots and Hasidism was no longer a force to contend with. Only then did the Maskilim consider it "safe" to study Hasidism and to assess its contributions to Jewish culture.

The earliest of the Hebrew and Yiddish modern writers to have something worthy to say of Hasidism were the poet and storyteller Isaac Loeb Peretz (1851–1915), Micah Joseph Berdyczewski (1865–1921), and S. J. Onoichi (Salman Isaac Aronsohn, 1878–1947), who were all influenced by the romanticism of nineteenth-century European literature. These writers began to admire the faith of the Hasidim of old: their stress on individuality, their mysticism, and their high spiritual temperament. The truth is that art could never thrive on worldliness and worldly ideals. Sociological schemes and even the progress of science and technology were never appropriate soil for the growth of art. The Haskalah could persuade people, convince them with its logic, but it could never produce the juices that nourish creativity. Neither Zionism nor the Jewish trend of socialism found their reflection in Jewish art. The Haskalah lacked the warmth and the exultation to really lift up the spirit. It could promise nothing but worldly gains. Willingly or unwillingly Judaism's finest writers and painters had to return to the life of the ghetto that the Haskalah despised, to its pious ancestors and to the joys that only Hasidism in its early stages could bring to the Jew. There is not a single true Jewish work of art that glorifies the Haskalah and its movement. The true artist is never inspired by sociology or politics.

For the past five decades Soviet critics have been exhorting writers, painters, and composers to create works that will serve to disseminate socialism and communism, but fifty years of revolution have not produced in Soviet Russia one such work of art of any consequence. Much the same holds true for Zionism. Speakers at every world Zionist Congress deplored the fact that Jewish literature in general and Hebrew literature in particular have been unable to do justice to the greatest and most important chapter of modern Jewish history: the epic of Zionism, with its development, its early setbacks, and its triumphs. But the artists did not react. Sholom Aleichem was certainly a Zionist, but his literary creations did not deal with Zionism. S. Y. Agnon, the first Hebrew writer to win the Nobel Prize, who spent the most productive years of his life in Israel, wrote little about the Jews who founded colonies and kibbutzim, but about the Hasidim and other pious Jews in the villages of his native Galicia. Yiddish literature is primarily devoted to Hasidism, Jewish folklore, and the life of poor and humble Jews in the Diaspora.

The efforts of practical thinkers can bring forth heroes, but not creative artists. The wars and the political upheavals of the Middle Ages and the early modern era have left few artistic monuments. Tolstoy's *War and Peace* is not a novel about war or the peace that follows war; it is merely an account of the life and loves of a few aristocrats in Czarist Russia during the first years of the nineteenth century. Throughout the ages, genuine art has been confined to only two themes—love and religion.

Even though the artist may consider himself a rationalist or an atheist, religion still has an impact on his work. The genuine artist still draws his inspiration from the eternal truths of the relationship between man and woman, and between man and his creator. All this is true in every field of artistic endeavor, including the pictorial arts.

Ira Moskowitz is the son of a Hasidic rebbe and descended from generations of fervent Hasidic Jews. As many other artists of Jewish background, he literally began to draw and paint on the covers of his father's holy volumes. The forces that guide the fate of men brought Moskowitz to the Holy Land when he was still very young. The years he spent there had a profound influence not only on his life but also on his art. He seldom drew Halutzim, or "Shomrim," who drained swamps, planted eucalyptus trees and fought off the early Arab saboteurs. Almost all his artistic energy went into portraying the Mea She'arim, where the extreme Jews lived and worshiped. He felt by instinct that they were the only guarantee of immortality.

Ira Moskowitz is a born master of drawing. In our day when most artists emphasize color and stress a symbolism that requires commentaries and interpretation, Ira Moskowitz has put all his artistic energy into the magic of line and the exploration of form.

It is no accident that Ira Moskowitz was asked to compile an anthology of the world's best drawings. In this monumental endeavor, to which he has devoted many years, he was guided in his choice, not by conventional standards, but by his own feelings for art. It is no surprise to those who know him and his work that he is now publishing a collection of Jewish art derived from his own work. In his sketches he portrays religious Jews in the Diaspora and in the Holy Land, at prayer in the synagogue, in the Hasidic *shtibels,* or study houses, and in the *beth midrash.* Figuring prominently in his work are the Scroll of the Law, the ethrog and lulav of the Feast of Sukkoth, the ram's horn of Rosh Hashonah—in short, all the institutions and symbols that have preserved the Jewish people during two thousand years of exile and without which they could not even survive in their own homeland.

I do not in the least presume to be a critic of art, but I don't tire of looking at Moskowitz's drawings—his Jewish faces, his depictions of Jews at study, at prayer, and in discussions of Talmudic lore. Moskowitz is familiar with every feature, every wrinkle in the face of the devout Jew. In his work he has recaptured the religious view of God and of the world. It is comforting to know that our artists are returning in ever-growing measure to the roots from which we draw our life blood and to the spiritual soil from which we have sprung. Long after the artistic world will have rejected the rootless abstractions of the present epoch, people will enjoy these images that bear witness to the Hasidic heritage and its everlasting faith.

HASIDISM AND THE ARTIST

BY IRA MOSKOWITZ

FOR CENTURIES ART AND RELIGION HAVE BEEN CLOSELY INTERRELATED. Each partakes of our deepest emotions. Because of this, both artist and religious leader have been able to fulfill much of humanity's basic needs. Art in fact is a form of religion; it is creative, spiritual, and richly endowed with great powers.

I have long been stimulated by religion, at times even preoccupied with it. In my childhood a religious atmosphere predominated. Both branches of my family stemmed from a long line of religious leaders dating back to the great rabbinical schools of medieval France. My father was a grandrabbi; a lineal descendant of the *maggid* of Zloczov and a collateral descendant of some of the leading figures of the Hasidic movement. My mother was similarly a descendant of illustrious rabbinical families.

In my earliest memories I can recall hearing wondrous stories of miracles performed by these holy men. Naïvely I believed them all. In the

25

company of my grandfathers I felt especially close to God because both approximated for me an anthropomorphic vision I had conjured up. Often I became carried away by the prayers of my maternal grandfather whom I held in particular awe. Much of what he said was beyond my comprehension but his mysterious voice had a way of working deep within me.

We became very close. Together we went on many trips. I remember one particular wedding we attended when I was eleven years old. We took a train to Soumbor, then boarded a fiacre to complete the trip. Because it had rained all day we had much difficulty in plowing our way through miles of muddy roads. On the train I strained to see as much as possible through the wet windows. Even then my eyes thirsted for sights, places, things.

The celebration went on for days and I was very drowsy most of the time, watching events through a twilight of fatigue. But not wanting to miss a thing, I forced myself to stay awake. I had such strange feelings about the bride and groom who were so shy. I knew man and woman were forbidden to touch in public, something I learned from my father and mother. To give my father an object, my mother had to place it on a table. Yet because I knew that marriage involved a certain closeness, these taboos seemed extremely puzzling. From childhood to manhood we were not allowed to so much as look at a girl or woman. More than a glance was considered sinful. Now this wedding, while confirming these restrictions, set off in me feelings it has taken years to shed.

Before I was thirteen I had heard of a great sage, the Belzer rabbi. Many people traveled to Belz to see this saintly man and to receive his blessings. The tales told by returning visitors were always fascinating. I had always been eager to travel, and now the temptation of going to Belz prior to the High Holy Days became impossible for me to resist. Yet I was too young to be allowed to travel alone. I had to find a way to see this great rabbi. Although I knew it was wrong, I "borrowed" several leatherbound tomes from the synagogue and pawned them. The money I received was just enough for a one-way ticket to Belz.

Belz was about five hundred miles away. It was a small town crowded with many people from all over Europe. To me it was another world, as strange as my own town was familiar. This was the first time I was away from my family. Alone and without money, I was given a place to sleep, along with many other people, on a heap of straw in an antechamber of the great synagogue. Twice a day we were given bread handed to us through a kitchen window. But my discomfort comforted me. I felt I was paying the proper price for my experience. Presently all thoughts of home began to recede. I tried many times each day to catch a glimpse of the great rabbi as he made his rounds. Being small, I was able to squeeze into places too narrow or inconvenient for others.

The rabbi took his meals in a huge hall adjacent to his private apartment. I was among the crowd that hung back to watch him as he tasted each dish and passed it on. Suddenly I was lifted up by a stranger and passed from shoulder to shoulder until I got close to the *gabai,* the rabbi's major domo. He let me take a handful of this sanctified food, which is called *schraim*. This I shared with those who had helped me get to him. But a small portion I saved until I returned home a month later.

While I was still in Belz, my uncle, the grand rabbi of Stryj, came to visit. He found me in the synagogue and took me to the chief *gabai's* home where we became his guests. Here there were great comforts: feather mattresses into which I sank and lush feather cushions and covers. There was also plenty to eat.

But when my uncle left the *gabai's,* I too said good-bye. In a sense I was relieved to get away. Among the pilgrims and the crowds I actually felt more comfortable, and I found that the meager rations I received were also sufficient.

Another vivid memory of my visit to Belz was that of being able to present a *quitle* to the great rabbi. In order to get the *quitle* written by one of the many scribes, I first had to wait hours in a small, crowded vestibule. When my turn came I asked that the scribe write that I continue to be a good Jew and a good student of the Talmud, and a petition for the well-being of my family and all of Israel. When this had been done, I was again told to wait for an audience with the great rabbi. After several nervous hours I was finally ushered into his presence.

The *gabai* had to hold me steady as I handed the *quitle* to the rabbi, who quietly touched and blessed me. When this happened I felt as if there was a great light burning inside me. I left feeling inspired as never before, an experience I shall always retain.

My father was the chief rabbi of Turka, then a province of Galicia. When the war broke out in 1914 Turka was razed. We were forced to flee to Prague where we remained for a number of years. Returning to Poland during the early 1920s we settled in Stryj. There we lived in my maternal grandfather's house, which pleased me.

My father had many followers in America. As there was an urgent need for spiritual leaders, he was invited by his followers to settle in the United States. At first he was reluctant because he had to determine whether this would be the proper place for his wife and children. After a short visit he decided that it was. We arrived in New York in 1927 and went directly to the apartment my father had selected on his initial visit. It was situated in the Lower East Side, near both a synagogue and a yeshiva. My brothers and I were enrolled in the yeshiva the following day.

It was during this time that my interest in drawing and art became greatly heightened. Although drawing pictures or making images of people was not encouraged, I secretly began sketching different things. I loved to draw so much that in spite of guilt feelings, I could barely stand to be away from my materials. One day my uncle caught me drawing and scolded me. "Why are you wasting time? You're too old for such nonsense," he said. My father too berated me for drawing. He urged me to study the Talmud instead. He very much wanted me to become a rabbi.

Most of my early drawings were done in the synagogue. To me this was a place for all sorts of stimulating activity.

Within a year of our arrival in New York I enrolled at the Art Students' League, studying with the late Harry Wickey, who became my life-long friend. Before long the Wickeys invited me to live with them in their Cornwall Landing, New York, home, where I pursued my art studies. Through Mr. Wickey I met the late Samuel Golden of the American Artists Group, who saw my earlier sketches from the little old Lower East Side synagogue and suggested that I illustrate *Ethics of the Fathers,* a book he planned to publish. I was delighted with his suggestion, which at last gave me an opportunity to widen my experiences beyond the atmosphere of the Lower East Side synagogue where I had worked almost exclusively for the past two years.

In 1935 the town of Newburgh, New York, sponsored an exhibition of my work. Much was sold. This gave me the chance to travel; first to Paris, then to Israel, known then as Palestine. But what I imagined would be a brief visit turned into a three-year stay.

The best way I can describe my sojourn in Israel is to say that it was an unreal reality, a dream come true. The spirit of its people living in the face of continual physical and political hardships quickly overwhelmed me. But unfortunately my own physical condition soon began deteriorating. Because of my unanticipated lengthy stay, I could not afford to eat more than one meal a day. As a result my body grew weak. At this point thoughts of my maternal grandfather began plaguing me. He had gone to Jerusalem some years earlier in order, he said, to die. Would I prematurely follow in his footsteps? My grandfather's departure had left a tremendous impression on me. He had been the center of my universe. I remember my family pleading with him not to leave, but he was insistent. The community too had urged him to remain. Debates lasted for months before he finally did go. He needed a photograph of himself in order to obtain a passport but because such graven images were forbidden by law he refused to have one taken. To this day I am not sure how the problem was resolved.

The entire community accompanied him to Lemberg on the day of his departure. For the occasion they engaged a special private train. Although some close relatives went further than Lemberg, my mother would not permit me to. How I cried. I knew that this was the last time I would be seeing my grandfather. I soon began to envision his death. I saw God taking him under His wing and into His bosom. Afterward in the *heder*, I openly mourned his death. For three months he visited all the holy places. Then he became sick and died of the one disease most fitting to a man of his station: Choley Majim. According to the Talmud, many of Judaism's saints had died from this stomach disorder. His short illness and death proved to the townspeople that he did indeed sense that his time had come.

Because of my hungry state while in Israel, I too began entertaining fears of Choley Majim. My one daily meal consisted of bread, onions, and tomatoes, swimming in olive oil. This diet soon raised havoc with my digestive system. Frequently I'd walk over and around the hills of Jerusalem, my stomach half empty, yet feasting on the brilliant sights set so remarkably off in the shimmering heat. Once a week, however, on the Sabbath,

I was fed a decent meal in the home of the editor of the *Davar*, the major newspaper in Jerusalem at the time. I think this one luxury helped greatly to assuage my fears.

Of the several cities in Israel, Jerusalem held the most appeal for me. Here the Bible took on a sharper focus. I was not only able to identify more closely with famous biblical cities but also with many of the inhabitants who seemed to possess an almost mythical mystique. Existing as I did, on a semistarvation diet, I was occasionally fortunate to sell one of my drawings. I drew every day and everywhere I traveled. Since watercolors dried too rapidly in the severe heat, I used pencils and pastels. But I was able to complete many works there.

One evening as I was eating my bread and onions, a very large man entered my room. He asked if I spoke English. When I told him I did, he immediately hired me as his interpreter. Shortly after I accepted the job, we became fast friends. He was a Protestant missionary from Ohio, in Jerusalem on a yearly visit. He was a warm and generous person with great love for all peoples. He derived much satisfaction from taking photographs of the *Halutzim* (laborers) and later sending them the prints. We saw each other for several weeks. Together we went to many holy places and colonies. I once accompanied him at dawn to visit the tomb of Christ. There he stretched out for a few minutes and when he arose I noticed a look of profound inspiration on his face. On another occasion I went with him to the Amic where we were warmly welcomed and given food and shelter. In fact, wherever we went I saw an enthusiasm in this man that few others could rival.

My favorite places were Mea She'arim, the Wailing Wall, and Safad. I had been working in these areas for about a year when fierce rioting and violence broke out. But I did not let this deter me. I continued working every day, searching for places that might be safe. There were several narrow escapes, a few of which I was sure would be the last.

Mea She'arim ignited in me some of my deepest religious moments. It is the section of Jerusalem where the most devout Jews live and pray. The spiritual sincerity there has remained steadfast for centuries. On a more recent visit to Israel I was again pleased to find that this quarter still possessed the same religious fervor.

Viewing the Hasidic Jew in his true environs is an uplifting and fulfilling experience. There he walks in pride. There he belongs, as if in the vineyard of his father. The late John Collier, minister of the Bureau of Indian Affairs, often remarked how "at one" the American Indian was in his surroundings. In the same way the Hasidic Jew in his homeland remains a timeless phenomenon, clearly transcending both political and religious barriers that, either out of habit or apathy, so many of us today have helped create.

Kabalists Studying Kabalistic Books

Hasidic Jews Discussing Some Text of the
Talmud or the Commentaries

HONOR BESTOWED ON A YOUNG BOY BY PERMITTING
HIM TO DRESS THE TORAH

A SCENE OF PRAYER

The satin robe and fur hat are accepted by the Hasidim as holiday clothes. Originally the hats were worn by Polish nobility. However, as with many customs borrowed from Gentiles, a particular Hasidic style was often added.

PORTRAIT OF THE ARTIST'S FATHER, A WELL-KNOWN
HASIDIC RABBI

A Hasid Praying

Texts of the prayers are almost the same everywhere (there are Sephardic and Ashkenazi versions). Every rabbi has his own style of praying. Some delay morning prayers until late in the afternoon; others delay evening prayers until early the next morning. This is their way of expressing Hasidic individuality.

At the Wailing Wall after Years of Arab Possession

A Composite Picture Commemorating Israel's
Victory in the Six-Day War

Lulav and Ethrog

Although women, according to the law, are not obliged to bless the lulav and ethrog, they are very eager to attend this ceremony.

The ethrog or citrus fruit was brought to Russia and Poland from both the Holy Land and Greece. The fruit from the island of Corfu is well known for its beauty. Wealthy worshipers provide especially beautiful silver containers to hold their ethrogs.

DRESSING THE HOLY SCROLL AFTER A READING

It is the custom to adorn the Holy Scroll (Torah) with embroidered mantles as well as with silver crowns, breastplates, and pointers. The dressing of the Torah is a special privilege granted to members of the community who are especially active in the synagogue.

The Ceremony of Blowing the Shofar

The shofar (ram's horn) is blown at Rosh Hashanah and at the end of Yom Kippur. It is also customary to blow the shofar on every day of the month of Elul, except on the Sabbath.

The Rabbi of Belz

Among the rabbinic dynasties, the one from Belz was most famous. Hasidim visited Belz from all over Galicia, Poland, and the Ukraine. During the Hitler holocaust, the Hasidim of Belz rescued the rabbi Aaron and took him to Israel. Two of his followers sacrificed their lives to save his.

A Father Going to a Prayer House with His Two Sons

Teaching religion to children is one of the most sacred commandments of the Torah.

Scene in a Jerusalem Synagogue Presided
Over by the Rabbi of Ladi

HASIDIC JEWS CONTEMPLATING SOME DIVINE MATTERS

EARLY STUDY OF A HASIDIC JEW

A Synagogue of Jerusalem

This synagogue was destroyed by the Arabs during the 1948 war.

BUCHARIAN SYNAGOGUE, JERUSALEM

There are no Hasidim among Oriental Jews. They have their own religious societies. Religion is for them both a way of serving God and a way of life. The two aspects are often so closely tied that it is hard to know where one ends and the other begins.

Early Study for Etching of an Oriental Synagogue

Exodus of Oriental Jews from Old Jerusalem during the
War with the Arabs

YOUNG PEOPLE STUDYING THE TALMUD

Even though the Talmud is holy to all religious Jews, the study of it often evokes ardent disputes. The Talmud contains different opinions of different sages regarding the law. It has given Jews an opportunity for endless discussion.

The Hasidim

YESHIVA BOYS DISCUSSING THE TALMUD, AS WELL AS WORLDLY MATTERS

KABALISTIC STUDY SESSIONS

A Teacher in a Religious School (Heder)
Where the Talmud Is Studied

It is the custom of the teacher to walk around the room while his pupils sit at open volumes. He often has the entire text memorized.

STUDY OF THE TALMUD IN A YESHIVA

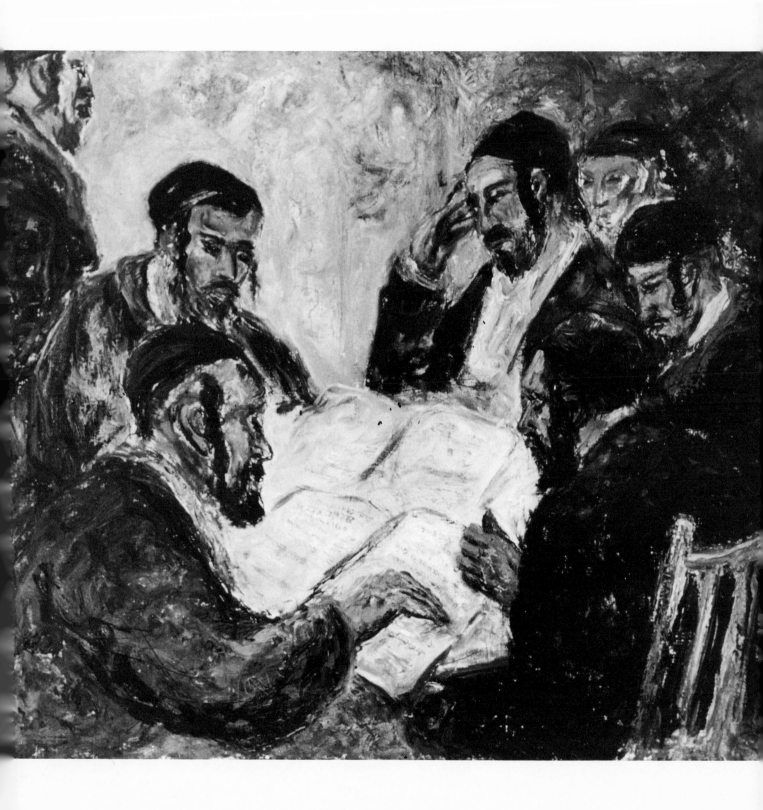

STUDY IN A SYNAGOGUE

PRAYER AND STUDY

Study

A Synagogue Scene

At the Reading Table

It is the custom that while the reader reads a section of the Holy Scroll, the members of the community look into the same text of the printed Pentateuch to make sure that he has made no mistakes in intonation.

PRAYER IN THE YESHIVA OF THE RABBI OF KOTZK

The Kotzk dynasty was as famous as the one of Belz, especially in Galicia, the part of Poland that once belonged to Austria.

Hasidic Jews in the Holy Land Praying in the
Yeshiva of Rabbi Meir, the Miracle Worker

A Saturday Afternoon at a Hasidic Prayer House

Prayer and study go together in Jewish religious life. In the Jewish faith, study is an integral part of the religion.

THE YOUNG AND THE OLD UNITED IN PRAYER

RELIGION GIVES HIM JOY AND ELATION

A Rabbi and His Followers

Some Hasidim Talking about a Miracle of the Rabbi, or Even Some Slight Gossip; Another Practicing the Shofar

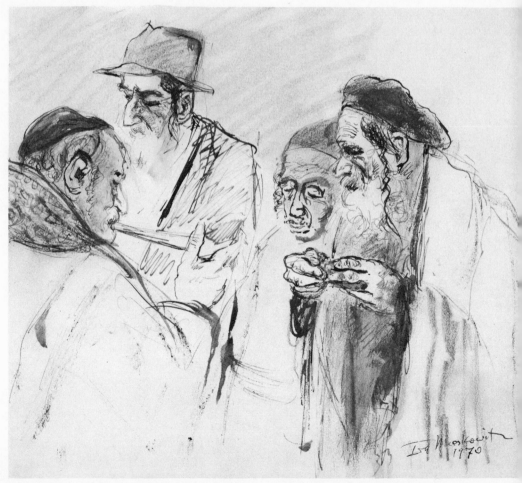

A Conversation among Hasidim

STUDY FOR AN ETCHING OF A HASIDIC PRAYER HOUSE

A FATHER ABOUT TO BLESS HIS SON ON THE
EVENING OF YOM KIPPUR

STUDY FOR ABOVE

CONVERSATION IN A SYNAGOGUE

It might be about the Torah or some other business. Hasidic study houses are used for many purposes: prayer, study, banquets, and routine matters. They are in many ways like clubs where members are free to indulge in whatever they please.

LATE HOURS AT THE YESHIVA

STUDY FOR THE RABBI OF BELZ

ONE JEW STUDYING, THE OTHER PRAYING

A Young Boy Learning to Put On His Phylacteries

A Bar Mitzvah Boy Being Called Up to the Torah

Study for an Etching of a Man Holding the Torah

Study for the Torah

HOLDING UP THE TORAH

Reading of the Holy Scroll

Only a small part of each chapter can be read. The Torah is read only on Mondays and Thursdays, in addition to the Sabbath and holidays.

Two Prayer Goers Rolling Back the Holy Scroll

When the reader comes to the end of the Scroll, it has to be rolled back to the beginning: the Book of Genesis. As a rule this is done at Simchas Torah.

PRAYER WITH THE ETHROG AND THE LULAV

CARRYING THE TORAH BACK TO THE ARK (A WEEKDAY)

On the Sabbath, phylacteries are not worn.

The Hasidim

STUDY FOR PRAYER WITH THE ETHROG AND THE LULAV

SKETCH RELATED TO THE ETHROG AND THE LULAV

STUDY OF A MAN WITH A LULAV

Two Hasidic Jews Have Just Bought Palm Branches and
Seem to be Happy with Their Purchase

Study of Jewish Wedding Musicians

Wedding Canopy

According to the Talmud, weddings are made in heaven. Forty days before children are born it is determined whose daughter shall marry whose son. Weddings are often occasions for Hasidic rabbis and their followers to get together and settle some Hasidic questions. There was once a Hasidic wedding attended by eighty rabbis—a combination of a wedding and a conference.

WEDDING CEREMONY WHERE MUSICIANS CAN BE SEEN

A Young Hasidic Couple

Hasidic Jewish women are not allowed to keep their hair after marriage. They wear bonnets, kerchiefs, and, in their later years, wigs. Brides shave their hair off just prior to their weddings. It is a sad day for many girls, but they comply all the same.

A WOMAN BLESSING THE CANDLES ON FRIDAY EVENING

Candles are always lighted before sunset to make sure that the Sabbath is not desecrated by creating fire or light.

BENEDICTION OVER THE WINE
DURING THE SABBATH OR ON HOLIDAYS

The head of the family recites the benediction and then the others are given a taste of the wine.

AN ELDERLY MAN AND HIS YOUNG WIFE

THE ARTIST'S UNCLE, WHO STILL LIVES IN THE SECTION OF
JERUSALEM CALLED MEA SHE'ARIM

A SCENE IN THE ARTIST'S HOUSE

On Friday night his grandfather would recite the benediction over
the wine.

PRAYER AT THE WAILING WALL

Religious Jews consider praying at the Wailing Wall a high privilege. They believe that prayers recited at this wall are given greater priority in heaven. Many religious Jews travel to Israel under the most difficult conditions just to be able to recite prayers at this remnant of the Holy Temple.

An Early Drawing of the Section of Jerusalem Called
Mea She'arim (The Hundred Gates), Where the
Most Orthodox Jews Live

Rachel's Tomb

Pious Jews consider Rachel's Tomb to be almost as holy as the Wailing Wall. It is believed that Mother Rachel interceded for the Jews before the Throne of the Lord. To the pious Jew, Mother Rachel is the symbol of mercy. She forgave and prayed for all repentant sinners.

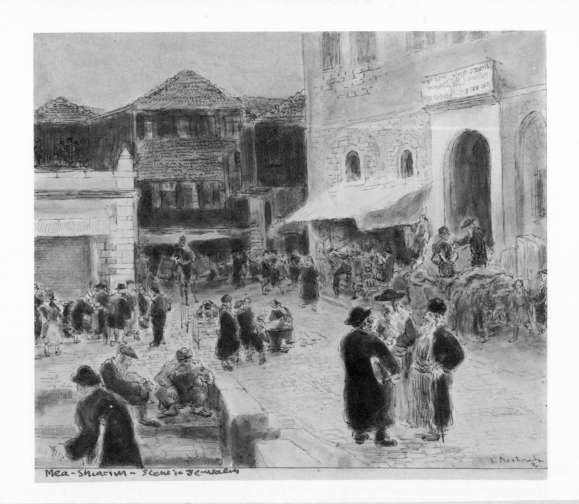

Mea-Shearim - Scene in Jerusalem

Old Jerusalem with Its Cupolas and Mosques

(This drawing was done from a rooftop)

THE OLD CITY OF SAFAD

Safad played a great part in the history of the Kabala. There lived the holy Isaac Luria and his disciple, Chaim Vital, who actually wrote Luria's books. The most famous of these books is *The Tree of Life*.

A Woman Praying at the Wailing Wall

Prayer and Study

The Wailling Wall

Ira Moskowitz
Jerusalem
1938

Some Still at Prayer, One Already Leaving

LEAVING THE SYNAGOGUE

GOING HOME AFTER THE SABBATH PRAYERS